Create Your Employee Handbook— Fast and Professionally

JOAN HARRIS

Asher-Gallant Press
Westbury, New York • New York

ABOUT THE AUTHOR

Joan Harris is a management consultant and a free-lance writer specializing in business-related subjects. She is a former personnel placement counselor and is currently the managing editor of *Home Business Magazine*.

© 1984 by Caddylak Systems, Inc. All rights reserved.

Library of Congress Cataloging-in-Publication Data

Harris, Joan.
   Create your employee handbook—fast and professionally.

  1. Employees' magazines, handbooks, etc. I. Title.
HF5549.5.C62H37   1986   658.4'55   86-3300
ISBN 0-87280-104-7 (pbk.)

Asher-Gallant Press is a division of Caddylak Systems, Inc. Address all inquiries to Asher-Gallant Press, 201 Montrose Road, Westbury, New York 11590, or call (516) 333-8221.

Printed in the United States of America

TABLE OF CONTENTS

Introduction 1
   How to Use This Book 1

Part 1—Planning and Organizing Forms 3
   Planning Form 5
   Outline Checklist 7
   Approval Memo for Employee Handbook Draft 11
   Approval Memo for Final Employee Handbook 12
   Approval Record 13

Part 2—Writing Aids 15
   Commonly Misused Words 17
   Transition Words 18
   Expressions to Avoid 19
   Wordy Expressions 20
   Punctuation Pointers 21

Part 3—Sample Employee Handbook 23
   1 About the Company 25
      Welcome 25
      What We Do 25
      Our Philosophy 26
      Our History 27

   2 How We Are Organized 28
      Organization Chart 28
      Major Departments and Their Functions 29
      Phone Directory 29

   3 Joining Us 30
      Employment Qualifications 30
      Equal Opportunity Statement 30
      Hiring Procedure 30
      How to Recommend a Potential Employee 31
      Keeping Our Records Current 32
      Seniority 32
      Relatives 32
      Transferring to Another Department 33

   4 Leaving Us 34
      Reasons for Termination 34
      How and When to Give Notice 34
      References and Recommendations 34
      Severance Pay 35

iv/Table of Contents

5 Evaluations, Warnings, and Probation 36
    Evaluations 36
    Probation for New Employees 36
    Warnings and Probation for Experienced Employees 36

6 Company Communications 38
    Your Supervisor 38
    Working with Other Departments 38
    Department Procedures That May Vary 39

7 Your Salary 40
    Time Cards 40
    Payday 40
    Payroll Deductions 40
    Raises 41
    Bonuses 41
    Promotions 42
    Pay Scales 42
    Expense Accounts 42

8 Days and Hours of Work 44
    Hours of Work 44
    Overtime 44
    Attendance and Lateness 45
    How to Report Absences 45
    Unavoidable Lateness 46
    Voting Time 46
    Bad-Weather Closings 46

9 Time Off 47
    Sick Leave 47
    Personal Days 47
    Emergency and Bereavement Leaves 48
    Paid Holidays 48
    Religious Holidays 48
    Vacations 49
    Long-Term Leaves of Absence 49
    Disability 50
    Layoffs and Recalls 51

10 Company Procedures 52
    Stationery and the Filing System 52
    Ordering Supplies 52
    Using Our Phone System 52
    Making Suggestions 53
    Handling a Problem or Filing a Complaint 53
    Printing Department 54

11	Company Rules and Regulations	55
	Code of Conduct	55
	Smoking	55
	Personal Calls and Mail	55
	Safety Regulations	56
	Right of Inspection	56
	Visitors	57
	Dress Code and Uniforms	57
12	Company Benefits	58
	Group Plans	58
	Health Services	60
	Tuition Assistance	60
	Company Loans	61
13	Special Services	62
	Food Services	62
	Welfare Committee	62
	Service Recognition	63
	Lost and Found	63
	Parking Lot	63
	Special Benefits	63
	Recreational Activities	64
	Company Parties and Events	64
14	Special Policies	65

Part 4—Reproducible Handbook Pages 67

INTRODUCTION

This book is designed to make it simple for your company to write an employee handbook. Such a handbook, or manual, is important for every company—large or small. It is the easiest, fastest, least expensive way to communicate to your employees your company's procedures, rules, expectations, goals, and philosophy. It is the best way to make sure your company is run smoothly and consistently. If you do not have a company manual, you probably spend a lot of time orienting each new employee, and a lot more time explaining procedures to your current employees over and over. You also waste a lot of time sending memos out every time an issue is misunderstood, a privilege abused, or a policy changed.

We recommend that one person (or a small committee) from the company be chosen to write the manual. A representative from the personnel department or a member of the administrative staff probably would be the best choice. It is important that the person send rough copies of each section of the manual to the appropriate department head or person in charge to make sure the information is correct. It is also important that the president or chief administrator read the entire book and approve its contents before it is printed or photocopied. Finally, you should have an attorney review the book, since policies stated in an employee handbook have figured in lawsuits by discharged employees. This book is illustrative and informative, not a definitive legal guide.

We also recommend that your company manual be put into a looseleaf binder. When you want to make a change, all you have to do is reprint the particular section and send it to your employees, rather than reprinting the entire book.

How to Use This Book

This book is divided into four parts. Part 1 provides forms to help you plan and carry out the writing of your employee manual. Part 2 gives writing pointers. Part 3, a sample employee manual based on an imaginary company, suggests what information to include and how to present it. Part 4 provides reproducible pages with typeset headings that will give your final manual a professional look.

Begin the project by turning to the **Planning Form** in Part 1. This is your blueprint for creating an employee handbook—just complete each step in the order given and the project will run smoothly. The other forms in Part 1 will help you obtain and organize the information for your handbook.

The writing aids in Part 2 will help you write clearly and simply and avoid errors in spelling, punctuation, and word usage. Review these forms briefly before you begin writing the manual and refer back to them if necessary as you write.

2/Introduction

When you have completed the first seven steps on the **Planning Form**, you are ready to start writing. Work section by section, using the **Outline Checklist** and the **Sample Employee Handbook** in Part 3. Decide which section to write, then read the corresponding section in the sample handbook. Rewrite that section to apply to your company. Pay special attention to the notes in the left-hand margin, which explain what information is important. By following the sample itself you will proceed easily and produce a clear, readable style of writing. The subjects in the sample manual have been organized logically to help you write the manual and to help your employees ultimately use it.

Finally, Part 4 includes pages that contain major section heads typeset attractively. You may use these pages, whether you photocopy or print the final draft of your employee manual, to give it a more professional look. If you are photocopying the manual, have the first page of each section typed onto a *photocopy* of the appropriate page in Part 4. If you are having the manual printed, have the first page of each section typed on standard typing paper, leaving room for the typeset heading. Take both the typed pages and the *actual* pages from Part 4 to a local quick-printer and have both the heading and the typed copy for the first page of each section printed together. Whether you photocopy or print the manual, use the typeset headings for the first page of each section only; type subsequent pages on blank, standard-sized paper. If you plan to put the handbook copies in three-hole binders, remember to leave a substantial left margin on each page. Also, photocopy or print the pages on one side only; this will simplify the future chore of replacing handbook pages as information changes.

PART 1
PLANNING AND ORGANIZING FORMS

PLANNING FORM

PAGE 1

DIRECTIONS: Check off each step as you complete it.

- [ ] Read through the **Sample Employee Handbook** in Part 3 to become familiar with the suggested contents of an employee handbook.
- [ ] Decide who will be responsible for planning and executing the project.
- [ ] Determine who will have the final authority to approve the handbook for company use.
- [ ] Determine the subject matter you want to cover. (You will find it helpful to review the **Outline Checklist** at this point. Check off the items you want to include and add any other areas you think should be included.)
- [ ] Have the outline reviewed and approved by the person or persons who will have the final authority to approve the manual.
- [ ] Determine which person or persons in your company is best qualified to give you information about each area you plan to cover.
- [ ] Interview these persons or send them questionnaires. (In either case, prepare the questions using the **Sample Employee Handbook** in Part 3 as reference. Be sure to encourage those responding to your questions to provide any additional information they feel is important.)
- [ ] Using the responses to your questions, begin writing the manual, section by section, using the **Outline Checklist** as a guide.
- [ ] Before writing a section, review the margin notes and sample for that section in Part 3.
- [ ] Take a break after writing the rough draft.
- [ ] Edit your draft.
- [ ] Prepare a table of contents.
- [ ] Have the draft typed, double-spaced.
- [ ] Proofread the typed draft.
- [ ] Determine who will review the draft for (1) content and accuracy, (2) **legal issues**, (3) quality of writing, and (4) general overview.
- [ ] Make a copy of the draft for each reviewer.
- [ ] Determine the deadlines you will be giving the reviewers.
- [ ] Send each reviewer a copy of the draft, along with a blank **Approval Memo for Employee Handbook Draft**.

PLANNING FORM

PAGE 2

- [ ] Use the **Approval Record** to keep track of who the reviewers are, what area each will be reviewing, and your deadlines.
- [ ] Phone each reviewer a few days before the deadline to remind the person that the deadline is approaching.
- [ ] Carefully consider all corrections, changes, and suggestions the reviewers have made.
- [ ] Make necessary changes on your copy of the draft.
- [ ] Have a final draft typed. (Use the typeset section headings in Part 4 for a professional look.)
- [ ] Proofread the final draft.
- [ ] Have any additional corrections made.
- [ ] Send copies of the final draft to the person or persons who have the authority to approve the manual for company use.
- [ ] Once approval has been given, have the handbook photocopied or printed.
- [ ] Put each copy of the handbook in a looseleaf binder.
- [ ] Distribute the handbook copies to all employees.

OUTLINE CHECKLIST

PAGE 1

DIRECTIONS: This outline will help you organize and write your company's employee handbook. Try to write sections in the order in which they appear on the outline, checking off each item within a section after you have written it. When you have completed all the items in a section, check off the section title. Proceeding in this way will help you focus on one topic at a time and will ensure that you do not omit any sections you want to include.

Refer to the corresponding items in the **Sample Employee Handbook** in Part 3 as you write. The margin notes will explain what information is important. The sample itself will serve as a model so that you can cover each subject in an easy-to-follow order and a readable, clear style.

- [ ] About the Company
    - [ ] Welcome
    - [ ] What We Do
    - [ ] Our Philosophy
    - [ ] Our History
- [ ] How We Are Organized
    - [ ] Organization Chart
    - [ ] Major Departments and Their Functions
    - [ ] Phone Directory
- [ ] Joining Us
    - [ ] Employment Qualifications
    - [ ] Equal Opportunity Statement
    - [ ] Hiring Procedure
    - [ ] How to Recommend a Potential Employee
    - [ ] Keeping Our Records Current
    - [ ] Seniority
    - [ ] Relatives
    - [ ] Transferring to Another Department

OUTLINE CHECKLIST

PAGE 2

- ☐ Leaving Us
    - ☐ Reasons for Termination
    - ☐ How and When to Give Notice
    - ☐ References and Recommendations
    - ☐ Severance Pay
- ☐ Evaluations, Warnings, and Probation
    - ☐ Evaluations
    - ☐ Probation for New Employees
    - ☐ Warnings and Probation for Experienced Employees
- ☐ Company Communications
    - ☐ Your Supervisor
    - ☐ Working With Other Departments
    - ☐ Department Procedures That May Vary
- ☐ Your Salary
    - ☐ Time Cards
    - ☐ Payday
    - ☐ Payroll Deductions
    - ☐ Raises
    - ☐ Bonuses
    - ☐ Promotions
    - ☐ Pay Scales
    - ☐ Expense Accounts

OUTLINE CHECKLIST

PAGE 3

- ☐ Days and Hours of Work
    - ☐ Hours of Work
    - ☐ Overtime
    - ☐ Attendance and Lateness
    - ☐ How to Report Absences
    - ☐ Unavoidable Lateness
    - ☐ Voting Time
    - ☐ Bad-Weather Closings
- ☐ Time Off
    - ☐ Sick Leave
    - ☐ Personal Days
    - ☐ Emergency and Bereavement Leaves
    - ☐ Paid Holidays
    - ☐ Religious Holidays
    - ☐ Vacations
    - ☐ Long-Term Leaves of Absence
    - ☐ Disability
    - ☐ Layoffs and Recalls
- ☐ Company Procedures
    - ☐ Stationery and the Filing System
    - ☐ Ordering Supplies
    - ☐ Using Our Phone System
    - ☐ Making Suggestions
    - ☐ Handling a Problem or Filing a Complaint
    - ☐ Printing Department

OUTLINE CHECKLIST

PAGE 4

- ☐ Company Rules and Regulations
    - ☐ Code of Conduct
    - ☐ Smoking
    - ☐ Personal Calls and Mail
    - ☐ Safety Regulations
    - ☐ Right of Inspection
    - ☐ Visitors
    - ☐ Dress Code and Uniforms
- ☐ Company Benefits
    - ☐ Group Plans
    - ☐ Health Services
    - ☐ Tuition Assistance
    - ☐ Company Loans
- ☐ Special Services
    - ☐ Food Services
    - ☐ Welfare Committee
    - ☐ Service Recognition
    - ☐ Lost and Found
    - ☐ Parking Lot
    - ☐ Special Benefits
    - ☐ Recreational Activities
    - ☐ Company Parties and Events
- ☐ Special Policies

APPROVAL MEMO FOR EMPLOYEE HANDBOOK DRAFT

DIRECTIONS: Please carefully read the attached draft of our company's newly developed employee handbook and review the specific area or areas checked below:

- [ ] content and accuracy of the following pages: _____
- [ ] legality
- [ ] quality of writing and clarity
- [ ] general overview

Please initial each page of the draft as you review it. You may mark specific comments, corrections, and suggestions directly on the copy (please use red ink). Use the space below to make general comments.

Please sign and return this form to _____ by _____, along with your copy of the draft.

Comments: _____

_____

_____

_____

_____

_____

_____

_____

Check one:

- [ ] I approve of the draft with no changes.
- [ ] I approve of the draft with changes as marked.

Signature _____ Date _____

Name _____ Title _____

APPROVAL MEMO FOR FINAL EMPLOYEE HANDBOOK

DIRECTIONS: Please carefully read the attached final draft of our company's newly developed employee handbook. Note that each section of the manual has been reviewed by the appropriate department head or person in charge to make sure the information is correct. The manual has also been reviewed from a legal standpoint and for the quality of its writing. By approving this final draft you will be authorizing the manual for company use.

Please initial each page of the draft as you review it. You may mark specific comments, corrections, and suggestions directly on the copy (please use red ink). Use the space below to make general comments.

Please sign and return this form to _____ by _____ , along with your copy of the final draft.

Comments: _____

_____

_____

_____

_____

_____

_____

_____

_____

Check one:

☐ I approve of the final draft with no changes.

☐ I approve of the final draft with changes as marked.

Signature _____ Date _____

Name _____ Title _____

APPROVAL RECORD

DIRECTIONS: Use this form to keep track of the different stages in the review process. First, list the names of those who will be reviewing the draft. Then, note what each reviewer is specifically responsible for (e.g., content and accuracy of a particular section or sections, legality, quality of writing, general overview). Record the dates the copies of the draft were sent and when you asked that they be returned. A few days before the deadline, phone the reviewers to remind them that the deadline is approaching. Then, record the dates the copies were returned and whether approval was given. Follow the same procedure for the final draft.

DRAFT APPROVAL

Name	Review Area	Date Sent	Deadline Requested	Date Returned	Full Approval	Qualified Approval	Comments

FINAL APPROVAL

Name	Review Area	Date Sent	Deadline Requested	Date Returned	Full Approval	Qualified Approval	Comments

PART 2
WRITING AIDS

COMMONLY MISUSED WORDS

affect — (v) to influence
effect — (v) to bring about, (n) result

all ready — prepared
already — previously

among — more than two involved
between — two involved

ascent — rise
assent — consent

complement — complete
compliment — praise

counsel — (n) advice, (v) to advise
council — (n) a group

device — (n) contrivance
devise — (v) convey

dyeing — coloring
dying — death

enforce — to compel
in force — in effect

exceed — to surpass
accede — to agree

farther — in space (best for distance)
further — in addition (best for time or quantity)

fewer — numbers
less — quantity

illicit — illegal
elicit — to draw out

loose — unattached
lose — to suffer loss

perquisite — privilege
prerequisite — requirement

precede — to go before
proceed — to begin or continue

principal — chief
principle — rule

stationary — fixed
stationery — paper

they're — contraction of they are
their — possessive
there — adverb, showing location

its — possessive
it's — contraction for it is

Also, do not use: **irregardless** for **regardless**
in regards to for **in regard to**
inflammable for **flammable**
very unique for **unique**
I as an object of a preposition (for **me**, not for **I**)

TRANSITION WORDS

INSTRUCTIONS: Use these words to help your work flow smoothly from paragraph to paragraph and topic to topic.

and	as a result
also	last
first, second	in conclusion
because	previously
since	formerly
further,	after this
next	now that
for instance	here
for example	to sum up
therefore	to illustrate
meanwhile	in another sense
as mentioned	at least
then	in fact
as suggested	comparable to
finally	yet
likewise	even
similarly	above all
however	consequently
on the other hand	only
nevertheless	otherwise
but	the former, the latter
in contrast	to repeat
although	again
therefore	once more
in summary	if

EXPRESSIONS TO AVOID

INSTRUCTIONS: Try to simplify your writing by replacing these redundant expressions and overworked cliches.

REDUNDANT EXPRESSIONS	SIMPLIFY TO
at a later time	later
after the conclusion of	after
until such time as	until
because of the fact that	because
by means of	by
for the purpose of	for
in order to	to
in connection with	with
continue on	continue
each and every	each
first and foremost	first
merged together	merged
proceed ahead	proceed
consensus of opinion	consensus
adequate enough	adequate
protrude out of	protrude
there is no doubt but that	no doubt or doubtless
few in number	few
thus as a result	thus
refer back to	refer to
each of these	each
have need to	need
inasmuch as	as
but nevertheless	but or nevertheless
first priority	priority
inside of	inside

CLICHES TO AVOID	REPLACE WITH
interface with	discuss
aforementioned	previous
pending determination of	until
pursuant to	about
opportunity to input	chance to contribute
utilization of	use
permit me to take this opportunity	I want to
thanking you in advance	thank you
foreseeable future	future, soon
acquiesce	agree
augmentation	increase
elucidate	explain
approbation	approval
would ask that	ask
has come to hand	learned
last but not least	last
venture a suggestion	suggest

WORDY EXPRESSIONS

INSTRUCTIONS: Review this list to determine if your writing is too wordy.

AVOID	REPLACE IT WITH
at the present time	now
as of this date; at that time	then
during the time that	when, during
at which time	
on the occasion of	
subsequent to	after
on the grounds that	because
as a result of	
owing to the fact that	
accounted for by the fact that	
by virtue of the fact that	
in spite of the fact that	although
with reference to	about
pertaining to	
in the event that	if
whether or not	whether
the question as to whether	
at an early date	soon
be in receipt of	get
owing to the fact that	since
come in contact with	meet
during the time that	while
come to a decision as to	decide
reach a conclusion as to	
make use of	use
be cognizant of	know
exhibit a tendency to	tend
give consideration to	consider
in close proximity	near
it is often the case that	often
make an examination of	examine
make mention of	mention
he is a man who	he
this is a subject that	this subject
after very careful consideration	after considering
is of the opinion	believes
make inquiry regarding	inquire

PUNCTUATION POINTERS

PERIOD

- Two typing spaces should follow the period at the end of a sentence.

- Use a period and one space after the initials of a name. Do not leave a space when the period is used as a decimal point in figures.

- Always put the period inside quotation marks.

QUESTION MARK

- If a sentence is part question, part statement, use the punctuation suggested by the final clause.

- Question marks are placed inside quotation marks only if they are part of the matter quoted.

COMMA

- Use a comma to separate two or more adjectives modifying the same word.

- Use a comma following an introductory phrase, before a direct quotation.

- Always put the comma inside the quotation marks, not outside.

- Items in series should be separated by commas. (It is permissible to omit the last comma before the conjunction.)

- Do not use commas if a clause is needed for complete understanding of the sentence.

- When in doubt, it is usually better to leave out the comma.

SEMICOLON

- Use a semicolon instead of a period if two sentences are closely related in thought.

- Use a semicolon instead of a comma when a comma would not make an adequate separation.

- Use semicolons to separate clauses if the clauses contain commas.

PART 3
SAMPLE EMPLOYEE HANDBOOK

1 | ABOUT THE COMPANY

Welcome

Explain what this book is about.

Welcome to Montana Communications!

We're sure you have many questions about the company and its workings: its procedures, its functions, and your role here. We've prepared this employee handbook to help answer these questions for you. You will want to keep this at your desk to refer to when you have questions or problems.

Provide positive reinforcement for the new employee about joining your company.

We feel sure that the company has made the right decision in hiring you, and that you've made the right choice in joining us. How do we know this? We think that after the exhaustive interview process, we've both had a great deal of time to evaluate each other and make a wise judgment. Further, we're proud to tell you that we have a turnover in personnel of less than five percent each year—a statistic that can't be matched anywhere in the industry.

Extend good wishes for the person's future at your company.

We hope you enjoy the challenge of working alongside Montana's two hundred employees. We wish you great success in your future here!

What We Do

Explain the basic concept of your company.

Montana Communications is a full-service communications company. That means we handle every communications function our clients may have. We are their full-service advertising agency. We are their public relations firm. We produce their training films and industrial films, as well as their television commercials. We handle their publicity. We design their brochures, booklets, letterheads, logos. We serve as their mail-order and direct-mail agency. We help them plan sales meetings, conventions, company parties, and special events.

Give an overview of how your company functions and what it produces.

Our writing and art staffs prepare all printed communications, including sales letters, annual reports, brochures, and a wide variety of advertisement formats. Our production department puts out commercials and short films. We have our own printing department, where we actually produce all materials developed by our creative departments. This includes our clients' stationery, brochures, reports, and even direct-mail pieces.

Because of the enormous amount of work produced for each client, and because of the founders' desire to maintain the special character that would be lost in a large agency, we have limited the number of clients we take on. We work hard to be all things to our clients, producing quality campaigns in all areas. We find it a very satisfying and successful concept of communications. Our clients agree.

These are the six corporations whose communications needs we handled as of September 1, 1984. We will send each employee a memo when any changes occur.

1. _____

2. _____

3. _____

4. _____

5. _____

6. _____

List all your clients or products or services. It is important that each employee is aware of your company's products and the way it operates, even though he or she might not be involved in every facet of work.

Our Philosophy

From the moment we opened in 1970, we have seen Montana Communications as a group of people working together to do an excellent job for our clients. Our success is due to hiring bright, talented people who work well together towards a common goal.

When our product doesn't seem up to par, we look to our teams to find out what went wrong. We make changes in the makeup of a team or teams, in our ways of motivating each other, and possibly in our creative approach. Rarely is one person expected to take the final responsibility for an error or a job we're not pleased with. And when we're proud of a campaign, seminar, training film, or other project, we congratulate the group (instead of an individual) for excellence.

Everything we do here is a team effort. Every person here is expected to do his or her job well. With the support we give each other and the excitement and enthusiasm we generate together, excellence never seems far from our collective reach.

In stating your philosophy, you have an opportunity to stress each employee's importance to the company.

You can motivate the employees by emphasizing that their performance is the key to the company's success.

When writing your company's history, be sure to include the date it started and who started it; its size at the beginning and its size now; the general concept and products, and whether those have changed since its beginning; and a statement on the company's plans to grow, develop, regroup, or move. You can also discuss the founders' backgrounds and how the company got its name.

Please join us in this team philosophy. It has worked well for us for all these years. Each person who works at Montana should know his or her importance to the company.

We are a company that is expanding, growing, and moving constantly on to new and different challenges. We can't do it without you!

Our History

Montana Communications opened its doors in May of 1970 in two small offices at 790 Main Street. It was started by Barbara Jean Montgomery, previously creative director for a major ad agency, and Bill Annenberg, an account executive for a public relations firm. They remain our two chief operating officers. The company is privately held, and Ms. Montgomery and Mr. Annenberg are its principal owners.

Montana—named for the state where both the founders grew up—began with one client and one philosophy: the idea that a company could handle, and handle well, all of a client's communications needs. Ms. Montgomery and Mr. Annenberg felt this was the only way an agency could give a client a consistent "look."

The idea was unique at the time, and, as with all new ideas, difficult to "sell." In 1973, however, Montana added a second client to the roster and thirty employees to the staff. From that time on, growth came quickly—almost too quickly. By 1978, with six clients and a staff of two hundred people, Ms. Montgomery and Mr. Annenberg made an important decision: the office was about as large as they wished it to grow. They decided that to maintain the innovative quality of the agency's award-winning work, as well as Montana's "small company" feeling, would be impossible if this office expanded much further. Their plans for growth, therefore, include other offices in other cities (a Chicago office is in the works for 1987).

2 | HOW WE ARE ORGANIZED

Organization Chart

Show an organization chart for your company.

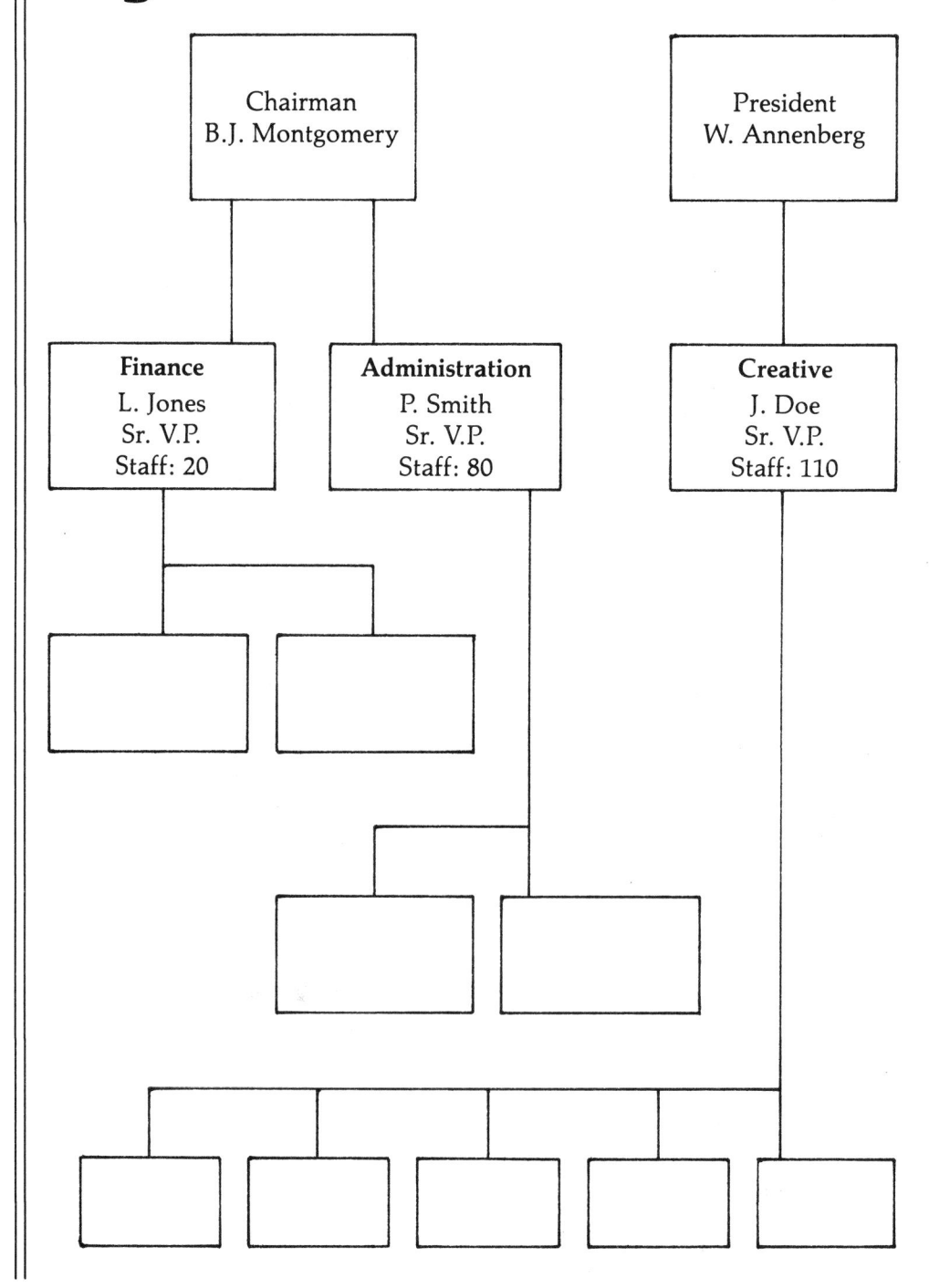

```
         Chairman                              President
      B.J. Montgomery                        W. Annenberg


    Finance          Administration            Creative
    L. Jones           P. Smith                 J. Doe
    Sr. V.P.           Sr. V.P.                 Sr. V.P.
    Staff: 20          Staff: 80               Staff: 110
```

Major Departments and Their Functions

List each department and give a brief description of its functions, as well as a general idea of its structure.

Department	Functions and Responsibilities
Accounting	Responsible for keeping track of monies billed, collected, loaned, and spent (any financial function except payroll). The head of this department is a senior vice-president.
Payroll	Responsible for issuing payroll checks and handling associated records.
Printing	Responsible for printing all brochures, proposals, stationery, direct-mail and mail-order campaigns, and annual reports. This department has a different schedule than the rest of the office, and its members are members of the Printers Union.
Traffic	This department is responsible for the scheduling of every campaign from preproduction through postproduction. It is made up of a traffic manager and twelve traffic coordinators (two for each of our six client groups), as well as four traffic assistants who keep the main schedules for all work produced.
Creative Groups I–VI	Each client has a unified creative group assigned to it. Each group is supervised by a creative director and has two senior art directors and two senior copywriters as well as a junior art and copy staff, which varies in size depending upon the volume of work required.
Management Services	This department handles support services used company-wide, including personnel, data processing, and research.

Phone Directory

Provide an alphabetical phone directory. Give employee's department and phone extension as well as his or her full name.

Name	Department	Extension
Adams, Ellen	Printing	124
Braverman, Alan	Payroll	221
Connors, Else	Accounting	191
David, Erica	Finance	137 & 138

3 JOINING US

Employment Qualifications

At Montana Communications, we have strict though simple guidelines to judge a candidate's qualifications for employment here.

Because we try to promote from within, we insist on the following qualifications for each employee hired:

1. You must have education or experience commensurate with the job.
2. You must be interested in a career with us and in communications—rather than just looking for a job.

Once we're assured that a candidate has those two qualifications, we work to determine whether his or her interests, aptitudes, skills, and experience fit the position to be filled.

Explain your reasons for qualifications.

List necessary qualifications.

Equal Opportunity Statement

We hire and promote employees on the basis of their qualifications, without regard to race, religion, color, sex, age, national origin, or a disability unrelated to the job in question.

This statement is important to include in any policy manual.

Hiring Procedure

In order to be considered for employment at Montana Communications, each prospective employee must:

1. Receive and fill out an employment application. These can be obtained by calling the personnel department, extension 100.
2. Meet with a personnel interviewer for a first conversation.
3. Once the interviewer feels the candidate's qualifications are right for a position, he or she will set up an appointment for the candidate to meet the head of the department the position is in. At this point, the personnel

State your procedure. Be specific as to the order of each step so that candidate will know what to expect.

department will request and check two business and two personal references. At this point, an offer can be made. However, for any position where the salary is above $22,000, steps 4 and 5 are necessary:

4. Should the department head be interested in hiring the candidate, he or she will then set up an appointment for the candidate to meet with a senior vice-president.

5. At this point, if the candidate, the department head, and the vice-president are certain the "fit" is right, a meeting will be set up for the candidate to meet with two people in the department. This will enable the candidate to further explore the workings of the department and get a better understanding of its work tempo and its personalities.

6. Once all involved are in agreement on hiring, the prospective employee undergoes a physical with our company physician.

7. If the applicant passes the physical, a written offer is sent.

8. If the applicant desires, he or she can request one more meeting with the prospective department head to discuss the offer.

9. The candidate is required to call Personnel to formally accept or reject the offer within ten days of receiving the offer letter.

How to Recommend a Potential Employee

Explain why you want (or don't want) your employees to recommend others.

At Montana Communications, we encourage employees to recommend people for possible employment. Because our employees are so familiar with our company and its needs, we know your recommendations will often be on target.

Describe any incentive you may offer.

We are so desirous of your recommendations, in fact, that we award $100 to a person who has recommended a new employee when that employee starts work here.

Explain the procedure for recommendations.

Each week, lists of all job openings are posted on the bulletin boards in front of the personnel department and in the hallway leading to the cafeteria. If you know someone who you feel would qualify for any of these positions, please pick up an application for them at the personnel office. Ask the candidate to fill this out and mail it to the personnel office. Ask them to make sure to put your name as a referral on the application.

Please do not try to "short-circuit" this procedure by recommending this person to a manager or vice-president.

Keeping Our Records Current

Explain what changes you require employees to report and who they should report them to.

It is important that your employment records are kept up-to-date. Be sure to notify the personnel department if there are changes in any of the following:

1. Your name.
2. Your home address.
3. Your home telephone number.
4. Your marital status.
5. The phone number where you can be reached in case of emergency.
6. The number of your dependents.
7. The beneficiary for your group life insurance, company profit sharing, or other benefit plan.
8. Your military status.
9. Your educational status.
10. Correction to your social security number.
11. Additional training, courses, or experience.

Seniority

Explain how seniority is determined and what it affects.

Your seniority is the length of continuous employment since the first day you started to work at Montana Communications. Seniority is a primary factor in deciding layoffs and recall and the length of your vacation, and may affect promotions.

Explain how and why seniority can be terminated. State any special regulations.

Seniority will be terminated when an employee quits or is fired for cause. The length of a company-approved leave of absence is deducted from your seniority.

Relatives

State policy.

It is our policy not to hire husbands, wives, or children of our employees.

List exceptions, if any.

An exception to this rule is made when two employees marry one another.

Transferring to Another Department

Explain why an employee might want to transfer to another area.

Explain how employees should request a transfer and what they can do if the request is denied.

Explain how transfer might affect seniority or salary.

Indicate that there might be differences in procedures from one department to another.

Transfers from one department to another occur frequently at Montana Communications. Many of the skills and talents required to complete various functions here are similar, and employees may want to broaden their experiences by transferring to another area. Often, employees are simply unable to work with one another. We recognize that personality conflicts can adversely affect a whole department's performance.

To request a transfer, you must speak with your supervisor. If you both agree that a transfer is advisable, he or she will work one out. If your supervisor is against a transfer but you're still sure it's the right move, you may schedule a confidential appointment with a personnel officer to discuss your feelings.

A transfer from one department to another does not affect your seniority with the company. It also will not affect your salary level at the time of the transfer, although a future raise may be agreed on at the time of the transfer.

Once you've transferred from one department to another, it's important to acquaint yourself with any differences in procedures in the new department.

4 LEAVING US

Reasons for Termination

An employee will be subject to discharge for the following reasons:

List reasons an employee may be fired.

1. He or she cannot do satisfactory work after a fair amount of time on the job and sufficient instruction.
2. He or she demonstrates frequent lateness or absences without acceptable reason.
3. He or she violates the code of conduct explained later in this manual.

Termination will only result after the warning and probation cycle explained in the next section of this manual.

How and When to Give Notice

State who to give notice to, how much notice you expect, and if you require it in writing.

If you plan to leave Montana, please try to give your supervisor at least two weeks' notice in a written memo. We request the two weeks as a courtesy to us to give us time to find a replacement for you.

References and Recommendations

State your company's policy on letters of recommendation.

It is acceptable to ask your supervisor for a letter of recommendation once you have given him or her written notice that you plan to leave. It is entirely your supervisor's decision, however, as to whether he or she will write such a letter.

Should you want other managers to write letters of recommendation for you, that is their decision as well.

It is also permissible for you to ask our personnel department to write a letter that details your job history with us: your length of stay, the dates, your salary history, and your exact job description.

Explain under what circumstances an employee might receive severance pay, who makes the decision as to whether the employee is granted the pay, and how much severance pay is given.

Severance Pay

Severence pay is granted to an employee who has been laid off or terminated because his or her services are no longer needed. If an employee is fired for poor attendance, incompetence, or other reasons where he or she is clearly at fault, severence pay is generally not given. The amount of severance pay is one week for every six months' service, with a minimum of two weeks.

5 | EVALUATIONS, WARNINGS, AND PROBATION

Evaluations

State when and how often employees are evaluated and by whom.

The job performance of each employee is formally evaluated twice a year (May and November). Your immediate supervisor will fill out the evaluation form, and you will receive a copy. At this point, you will have a meeting with your supervisor to discuss the evaluation.

Explain what these evaluations can mean to the employee.

These evaluations affect your promotions, raises, and year-end merit bonus.

Explain how an employee can appeal an evaluation he or she thinks is unfair.

If you believe your evaluation is unfair, you may schedule a meeting with a personnel official or with senior management to discuss it.

Probation for New Employees

Explain the probation period for new employees.

All new employees are considered to be on probation for the first three months of their employment. Your supervisor will evaluate your work after six weeks and again at the end of the three-month period. The evaluations will be discussed with you, and Personnel will receive a copy. If your work is unsatisfactory, your supervisor, after consulting with the personnel department, can dismiss you after three months or extend the probation period another six weeks.

Warnings and Probation for Experienced Employees

Explain the steps taken by management when a more

Employees no longer on probation whose work appears below standard will receive a first, or oral, warning from a supervisor. This warning will not be reported to management or Personnel. If, two weeks after receiving

36

Evaluations, Warning, and Probation/37

experienced employee's performance is not satisfactory.

Be specific on both the length of probation and who makes the final decision.

State any avenues of appeal employees have within the company.

this warning, the supervisor remains dissatisfied, he or she will send you a written warning, with a copy going to Personnel and to senior management. Two weeks after this written warning, your supervisor must inform Personnel, again in writing, whether your performance has improved or whether you should be put on probation.

Your probationary period will last four weeks. You will be reviewed by your supervisor after two weeks and after four weeks. On the last evaluation, your supervisor has the option of dismissing you.

You will receive copies of all reports involved, and your supervisor will meet with you to discuss each evaluation. You may request a meeting with officials from the personnel department or senior management during the probationary period to discuss any special difficulties.

6 COMPANY COMMUNICATIONS

Your Supervisor

Describe the functions of a supervisor.

Your supervisor is the person to turn to with your problems, questions, criticisms, and suggestions. He or she is fully responsible for the day-to-day running of your department or section. He or she is at least partially responsible for its workload and flow, yearly budget, hiring, firing, and growth.

Explain how and when to communicate with supervisors.

Every two weeks, all supervisors meet with their entire department to discuss the previous two weeks of work and the upcoming two weeks, as well as to iron out problems, hear suggestions, determine priorities and, specifically, to listen to you. Of course, supervisors are receptive to employees' problems at other times as well.

Here is an opportunity to stress your company's philosophy with regard to employees working together.

We stress communication here: talking it over; talking it out; listening to each other; respecting each other's abilities, talents, and difficulties. It works!

Working with Other Departments

This section is another policy statement. Explain to your employees whether you want them to have direct contact with other departments or if such contacts should be made through supervisors.

Montana Communications has many varied departments and work groups. Consult your list of departments and their functions at the beginning of this book. This will suggest to you who to contact with regard to special problems or questions.

Although your supervisor can direct you to the right department to get an answer, feel free to acquaint yourself with the functions of the various departments and the people who work there.

We encourage you to get to know each department. At some point, you will probably need to talk to someone in every other area here.

Department Procedures That May Vary

Explain any variations in regulations, schedules, etc., in different departments or areas if they exist within your organization.

Several of our departments, due to their specific functions, have regulations, schedules, and working styles that vary from the company standard. These variations are explained under "Hours of Work."

7 YOUR SALARY

Time Cards

Explain when time cards are due, what information is necessary, and what can happen if cards are not handed in on time.

Every Monday, each employee will be given a time card to turn in to his or her supervisor at the end of the week. Hourly employees—who include clerical workers and some junior professional, technical, or supervisory staff members—must fill in all hours worked and lunch, personal, and sick time taken. Exempt employees—employees whose time is not figured by the hour and who are not eligible for overtime—simply indicate any sick leave or days off taken. If a signed card is not turned in on time, the payroll department cannot issue a check.

Payday

State what day is payday.

You will receive your salary check every Wednesday morning.

If Wednesday is a holiday, the checks will be handed out on the preceding Tuesday afternoon.

We make every effort to get the salary checks to you on time each week. On rare occasions, however, we do have a computer breakdown. We apologize for any inconvenience this may cause.

Explain what to do in the event of a lost check.

If you should lose your check, report it to the payroll department immediately.

Explain how to obtain your check if you are absent on payday.

If you are not at work on Wednesday, your supervisor will hold your check until you return to work.

Payroll Deductions

State which deductions are made and why they may vary.

Federal, state, and local income taxes and social security payments, all required by law, are deducted from your weekly earnings. Often, these deductions may change as they are affected by changes in the amount you earn, by legislation, and by the number of dependents you declare.

List possible voluntary deductions.

You may authorize voluntary deductions for any of the following:

   Stock Option Purchase Plan

   Retirement Plan

   Credit Union

   Supplementary Insurance Plans

Explain who to call with a question about deductions.

If you have questions about the deductions which appear in your weekly statement, call the payroll department.

Raises

Explain to employees how raises are figured, when they are awarded, and how notification is made. Be sure to spell out whether new employees are eligible for standard yearly raises.

Each employee receives an annual salary increase. One component of the raise will be a standard cost-of-living increase given to everyone in the company. The other component of the raise is a merit increase. Its size depends on the quality of your work during the preceding year and the contributions you have made to your department and to Montana Communications.

Raises will be decided on by your supervisor and by senior management in December of each year, based primarily on your performance evaluations. You and your supervisor will meet to discuss your raise just before the Christmas holiday. Raises take effect January 1.

Raises generally are not given except at the first of the year. The exceptions are midyear promotions and transfers.

New employees must have completed their three-month probationary period by December 15 to receive the annual raise. New employees whose probation is extended and other employees who have been placed on probation because of unsatisfactory performance will have their raises discussed after the probationary period is completed.

Bonuses

Explain the company's policy on bonuses, if any.

Montana Communications also gives employees an annual Christmas bonus. Employees of more than one year's service receive between one and two weeks' pay, depending on responsibility and performance. The amount of your bonus will be discussed with you at the time you are told of your annual raise. Bonus checks will be distributed on the last working day before Christmas.

Explain factors involved in promotions and how an employee may apply for one. Indicate the person or group of people who decide on promotions.

Promotions

The company makes every effort to promote from within. Before filling any position from outside, we look carefully at any current employees who may, with guidance and perhaps some additional training, be qualified to hold it. Supervisors may recommend employees for promotion, and employees are encouraged both to apply for specific openings that may occur from time to time and to let management know, in general, if they are interested in career advancement. Employees are especially encouraged to enroll in courses or seminars that will broaden their qualifications and to report the successful completion of those courses to management. The supervisor of the affected department has a key role in selecting an employee for promotion, although senior management makes the final decisions.

Pay Scales

Explain how the pay scale is determined and assigned to each job.

We have tried to assure that our employees will receive equitable compensation. We have set up a system for grading all jobs in relation to other jobs in the company. We considered the requirements, initiative, responsibility, and conditions of each job.

Explain to the employees how they can progress upwards within the scale assigned to their position.

Each job is assigned a salary grade based on these factors, and each position is given a salary range. Your individual progression within this salary range is based upon your performance and the amount of time you have worked for the company.

Say where employees can get answers to questions about the pay scale. Indicate whether the company considers salary information confidential.

If you have a question about where you fall on the salary scale and why, feel free to make an appointment with your supervisor to discuss it. We will do our best to answer your questions candidly. We do, however, consider salary information confidential, and we request that you do not discuss your salary with colleagues, clients, or competitors.

Expense Accounts

Explain the following: which employees have expense

Your supervisor will explain the extent and use of any expense account privileges to you. You may be given a company credit card to be used for approved business expenses only.

accounts, what forms they must fill out, when to fill them out, when they are due, when the monies will be reimbursed, what approval is required, where to submit forms, and what receipts are required.

If you have an expense account, you must submit an expense account form (EA 1) by the 30th of each month. Your department secretary will hand out these forms each month. Attach all credit card receipts to this form as well as receipts for out-of-pocket expenses exceeding $15. Have your supervisor sign the form before sending it to the accounting department. You will be reimbursed within a week. Any forms received after the 30th of the month are processed the following month.

Any expenses incurred by employees while traveling on company business must be noted on a travel expense form (TA 1). These forms are available through your department secretary. Travel allowances are specified on each form, so it is necessary to obtain a form in advance of your trip. Each travel expense form must be filled in, signed by your supervisor, and sent to Accounting no later than four working days after your return.

8 | DAYS AND HOURS OF WORK

Hours of Work

Specify normal work hours and days, lunch hours, and coffee breaks.

The standard company workday starts promptly at 9 A.M. and ends at 5:30 P.M. Our week goes from Monday through Friday. Hourly employees are given an hour for lunch each day, which must be taken between the hours of noon and 2 P.M. If you need extra time, make arrangements with your supervisor in advance. Every employee is given two fifteen-minute coffee breaks each day: one in the morning and one in the afternoon. Your supervisor will advise you as to when you may take these breaks. Some departments take their breaks together, while others stagger the times.

Note exceptions. Be specific to avoid confusion.

Here are the exceptions to the standard working hours:

1. The mailroom staff works on two daily shifts. The morning shift works each day from 7 A.M. until 3 P.M. The afternoon shift starts work at 1 P.M. and works until 9 P.M.

2. The printing department starts work at 8 A.M. each day and works until 4 P.M. At 4, a part-time crew arrives to work the presses until 8 P.M.

3. All receptionists work from 8 A.M. until 4 P.M., with a one-hour break for lunch from noon to 1 P.M. During this lunch break, the department secretaries on each floor are responsible for the reception areas on a rotating basis. Those assignments will be handed out to the secretaries by a supervisor each Monday morning. A part-time reception staff arrives every day at 3:30 and is responsible for answering the phones and accepting deliveries until 8 each evening.

After 8, the doors will be locked. If you must stay and wait for a package, the night elevator operator can accept this for you and buzz you on the intercom to come to the front door.

Explain why changes in schedule may occur and how employees will be notified.

Should there be a change in the day's work schedule, due perhaps to holiday hours or to early closing for bad weather, we will let you know, by memo, as soon as possible.

Overtime

Make clear when overtime begins and whether it is

Overtime is a constant necessity in the communications business, and employees are expected to be able to work overtime when the need arises. Hourly employees may work overtime only with the approval of their su-

necessary to have approval to work overtime. Let employees know if overtime will be expected regularly. Say whether compensatory time is permitted.

pervisor. You begin working overtime after you've worked a minimum of forty hours in a regular work week. You are paid overtime at the rate of 1½ times your basic straight-time hourly wage. If you desire and your supervisor approves, you can take overtime as compensatory time off, at a straight-time rate.

Specify who can collect overtime pay.

Only hourly employees and some junior professional or technical staff members are eligible for overtime. For supervisors, managers, and senior technical and professional staff, overtime is considered a hazard of the profession. Your initial offer letter will have made clear whether you are eligible for overtime.

Attendance and Lateness

Stress promptness and consistency.

We expect each of our employees to report to work on time and to continue to work until the end of the workday.

State how poor attendance can affect employees.

An unsatisfactory attendance report, frequent lateness, and long lunch breaks may be cause for probation. Should this continue, your attendance record could be reason for dismissal.

Your attendance record can be a significant factor in evaluating you for raises, promotions, and bonuses, and could be important in deciding which employees are laid off first.

How to Report Absences

Specify who to call—and how often to call—in the event of absence.

If you know you will be absent in advance, please tell your supervisor. If this isn't possible, please telephone your supervisor as early as possible on the first day of your absence. After that, call your supervisor daily until you are able to report for work again.

Explain what happens if employee does not follow correct procedure.

If we do not hear from you for three workdays, we will assume you have left your job.

Unavoidable Lateness

Explain what employees should do when they must be late, or lateness is unavoidable.

If you must be late for work, or need extra time for lunch, please clear this with your supervisor.

We realize, of course, that lateness sometimes cannot be avoided. Please report directly to your supervisor to explain should you arrive late. If your supervisor is not available, report to the department secretary.

Voting Time

State who may be permitted to take voting time with pay, in what elections, and how much time off is allowed.

You may take time off with pay to vote in a federal or state election only if you would be unable to reach the polls otherwise. Please advise your supervisor in advance that it is necessary for you to take this time off. We ask that you do not miss more than one hour of work in order to vote.

Bad-Weather Closings

Explain procedure to follow to find out about closings and what employees should do if they cannot get to work due to weather conditions.

To find out whether the office will be open in bad weather, tune to either WLOV-FM or Cable TV Station 22 between 6 and 9 in the morning.

Should Montana not be listed as being closed, yet you are sure you will be unable to get to work, call your supervisor.

State conditions under which employees are paid for time off due to bad weather.

If the office is closed because of bad weather, you will be paid for the day(s), and the time off will not be considered a personal day or a sick day. However, you will not be paid for the day(s) if the office is open but you cannot get to work due to weather conditions. In this case, the time off will be considered a personal day.

9 TIME OFF

Sick Leave

> **Explain when employees begin to earn sick leave, and indicate whether the number of days grows with length of service. If sick leave is awarded on an annual basis, say whether it is cumulative from year to year.**

Sick leave for employees with less than two years of service is awarded as follows:

0 to 3 months	3 days
3 to 6 months	5 days
6 to 12 months	10 days
12 to 18 months	15 days
18 to 24 months	20 days

(Totals after 3 months are cumulative days)

> **Warn employees against abusing sick leave and indicate the consequences.**

After two years of service, employees receive unlimited sick leave. We expect, however, that employees will not abuse the privilege. Employees found to be abusing sick leave will be considered to have been absent excessively and therefore may be liable for probation and possible dismissal.

> **Remind employees how to report sick. Tell them whether they need a doctor's note when they return to work.**

Employees are expected to call their supervisor each day until they return to work. If you are out sick for more than five days, please bring a note from your physician when you return.

Personal Days

> **If your company gives personal days, explain how many and their purpose. Tell employees how to schedule them.**

The company gives employees with at least one year of service one or more personal days. You may use these as vacation days or for such errands as doctors' appointments. Personal days are awarded on the following basis:

after 1 year	1 day per year
after 2 years	2 days
after 3 years	3 days
after 5 years	4 days

You must schedule personal days off in advance with your supervisor.

Emergency and Bereavement Leaves

Explain whether your company allows such leaves, their length, under what circumstances they are granted, and whether all employees are eligible.

The company will give any employee up to three days off with pay in the case of the funeral of a close relative (normally defined as parent, child, spouse, brother, sister, grandparent, or other relative the employee has lived with) or in an overriding personal emergency involving an employee or a member of the immediate family. If you cannot let your supervisor know in advance that you need such a leave, please contact him or her at the earliest possible opportunity.

Paid Holidays

Montana Communications is closed for business on ten holidays each year. These are the only paid holidays we observe. They are:

List your holidays.

- New Year's Day
- Good Friday
- Memorial Day
- Independence Day
- Labor Day
- Thanksgiving Day
- Day after Thanksgiving
- Christmas Eve
- Christmas Day
- New Year's Eve

Explain what is done if holidays fall on the weekend.

If a holiday falls on a Sunday, it will be observed on the following Monday. If it falls on a Saturday, it will be observed on the preceding Friday. We will announce these closings well in advance of the holiday.

Religious Holidays

Explain company policy on religious holidays.

The company respects the right of each employee to worship as his or her faith dictates, but for economic and competitive reasons we cannot observe religious holidays other than Christmas and Easter. Employees may apply personal days, vacation days, or accumulated overtime toward other religious holidays they wish to observe. Please make arrangements with your supervisor as far in advance as possible.

Vacations

State who is eligible for vacation and how much vacation time is awarded.

After six months of service, you are entitled to one week of vacation with pay. One year of service entitles you to two weeks' paid vacation. After five years, you will be entitled to three weeks of vacation with pay.

Explain how to schedule vacations. Say whether seniority or first-come, first-served governs vacation dates.

Please schedule your vacations with your supervisor as far in advance as possible. We ask that, when possible, you schedule your vacation in one-, two-, or three-week blocks. Vacation slots are filled on a first-come, first-served basis.

Any special vacation policies should be stated here.

We offer, as a bonus, an additional two days' vacation each year to each employee with a perfect attendance record. Personnel will notify you by memo if you have qualified for this bonus.

Explain what happens to unused vacation time when an employee leaves.

If you leave Montana Communications before taking the entire vacation time due you, you will be paid for these days (at a straight-time hourly wage) as long as you have given the company at least two weeks' notice in writing.

Long-Term Leaves of Absence

Explain what a long-term leave is, length of time and possible reasons for leaves, how an employee should request a leave, and who can give the approval.

A long-term leave of absence consists of more than five working days when you cannot be at work for reasons other than illness. To apply for such a leave, fill out an application and submit it to your supervisor. Please make sure you are aware of the specific regulations concerning the type of leave you will be taking. Check with Personnel if your particular reason for a leave is not discussed here.

Note any insurance specifications.

Premiums on insurance will be paid by the company during any of the following approved long-term leaves of absence.

Give the details on each kind of leave, including length of

Maternity Leave. Granted to a pregnant employee. It is necessary to submit a doctor's letter stating the last day you're permitted to work before delivery. This leave must end no later than six months following delivery. Em-

time allowed, whether employee is paid or not, and how to apply for the leave.

ployees with more than three years' service will be paid for three months; those with five years' service will be paid for six months.

Paternity Leave. Granted to a new father without pay for any ten weeks before, during, or up to eight months after the birth of his child. A doctor's letter stating the expected date of delivery must accompany the employee's application.

Military Leave. Granted to any employee who is a member of the U.S. Armed Services Active Reserve or National Guard for temporary field training or emergency duty. This employee will be paid his or her regular salary for the time absent (maximum of two weeks in any calendar year), minus the amount of military pay received for that period. Please submit a copy of military paychecks received to the payroll department (with a copy to Personnel) when you return to work. A military leave is considered separate from vacation time. However, you cannot take your vacation directly before or directly after this leave.

Jury Duty. When an employee is called to serve on a jury, he or she will be granted a leave of absence as long as he submits the jury summons to Personnel. An employee will receive his or her regular pay during this period, minus the amount paid for serving on the jury. When you return to work, you must submit to your supervisor a statement from the court detailing the dates you served and the amount you were paid.

Personal Leave. Should you need a long-term personal leave of absence, you must discuss the reason with your supervisor. Your supervisor must obtain permission from the chairman for you to take this leave. All personal leaves are without pay. They are limited to one year in duration.

Disability

Explain regulations concerning disability leaves: what forms and letters are required, what pay allowances are given and how they are determined.

Any employee who has worked at Montana for a minimum of one month may be granted a leave of absence for illness or injury. All leaves that are considered disability leaves require a doctor's letter explaining the reasons for the disability and the dates. Montana will continue to pay the employee's premiums for group insurance during the leave. The pay allowances while on a disability leave are based on an employee's length of service, as follows:

Length of Continuous Service	Maximum Pay at Full Pay	Allowance at 70% Pay
1-5 months	none	26 weeks
6 months-1 year	1 week	25 weeks
1-2 years	2 weeks	24 weeks
3-4 years	3 weeks	23 weeks
5-9 years	4 weeks	22 weeks
9-14 years	6 weeks	20 weeks
15 years and up	8 weeks	18 weeks

An employee who has taken more than two weeks' disability leave must bring a doctor's note to the personnel department stating he or she is now able to return to work without risk.

Layoffs and Recalls

In the case of a company or department layoff, explain the order and deciding factors involved.

Should a layoff be necessary, employees will be laid off on the basis of their length of service. If the length of service for two or more employees is equal, the next deciding factors are attendance and productivity.

State order of employees in a recall and how employees will be notified.

You will be recalled to work in the reverse order of the layoffs. You will be notified of the recall by registered mail. Should you not return to work within two days after a notice of this recall has been received, we will assume you are not planning to return.

Explain any effect a layoff might have on insurance premiums, stock programs, seniority.

During a layoff, the company will continue to pay all regular insurance premiums. Stock programs, pension funds, and seniority will not be affected.

10 COMPANY PROCEDURES

Stationery and the Filing System

Explain to employees which stationery and forms to use and when.

Because our company stationery is expensive (cream stock with an embossed company logo), we ask that you use it only when sending a letter outside of the company. We provide you with interoffice memo forms and plain white typing paper for all other uses. Memo paper is to be used only for interoffice correspondence. It is important that you send copies of your memos to anyone directly involved in the issue you are writing about.

Indicate any special format you require for letters and memos.

The company's preferred style for typing memos and letters is explained in the Secretary's Guide, handed out to all secretaries on their first day of employment.

State how many copies are to be made, and how and where to file them.

At least three copies are to be made of each piece of correspondence. One copy is filed in the department files; one copy will be filed chronologically in a looseleaf binder, kept on the department secretary's desk; and one copy must be sent to your supervisor. You may request an additional copy for your own records.

Ordering Supplies

Explain company procedure used when ordering supplies.

Office supplies, such as stationery, memo paper, typing paper, envelopes, carbon paper, pencils, pens, and typewriter ribbons, can be ordered only through your department secretary. Fill out a pink supply form (SF 1) in duplicate and give both copies to the department secretary in the morning. You should have your supplies by the end of the day.

Any requests for supplies not kept in stock must be approved by your supervisor. Fill out a blue supply form (SF 2) in duplicate and give both copies to your supervisor. He or she will either order the supplies or get you a check from Accounting so that you can buy them yourself. Make sure to give the Client Account Code, if applicable, when ordering any supplies.

Using Our Phone System

Explain how to make interoffice, local,

To make an interoffice call, simply dial the correct extensions (as found in your phone directory).

and long distance calls on your company's phone system. Include any special regulations you have.

If you have a special system or service, explain how to use it here.

To make an outside call, dial "9" before dialing the phone number. You can call anywhere in the New York State, New Jersey, and Connecticut by dialing direct, using the proper area code where necessary. To dial outside these areas, dial "0" for a company switchboard operator. Give the operator the phone number and area code you are calling, as well as the name and company name of the person you are calling. It is also necessary to tell the operator your name, your extension, and the account you are working on.

In addition to this system, we do have a WATS line to the following cities: London, Rome, Milan, Paris, Los Angeles, San Francisco, Chicago, Dallas, Detroit and Tokyo. To make a call to any of these cities, first dial 1-234-777-3, wait for a clear signal, and dial the area code and phone number. It is not necessary to report these calls. However, please do not use this WATS line for personal calls! Should the WATS line be tied up and your call cannot wait, dial "0" and give the number to the company operator.

Making Suggestions

Explain how employees can go about making a suggestion.

Do you offer an incentive for this? Explain how it works.

We truly welcome and encourage your suggestions on how to improve procedures, atmosphere, and productivity at Montana Communications. We offer a cash bonus when an employee's suggestion is put into use. In 1983, eight employees received bonuses ranging from $50 to $600.

Your suggestions may be submitted by placing them in the suggestion box located outside the personnel department. The best suggestions are forwarded by Personnel to a committee of senior managers that decides on awards.

Handling a Problem or Filing a Complaint

Explain how you would prefer to have employees deal with complaints or problems.

Explain the options an employee might have when dissatisfied with a solution or suggestion.

We encourage our employees to learn to talk things over when they have problems or complaints about job conditions or colleagues. Bring these matters to your supervisor's attention first. Should you feel that your supervisor's response does not solve your problem, you may make an appointment with a member of the personnel department. They are happy to work with you to try to solve problems, hear your complaints, and make suggestions. At your request they will be willing to set up an appointment for you to meet with the chairman or the president.

Explain how employees can use the services of any specialty departments. Be particularly detailed in the case of departments they may not have dealt with before when working in other companies.

Printing Department

Please try to hand all necessary material for printing to your traffic coordinator by 9 A.M. if you need it that afternoon, or by 3 P.M. to receive it by the next morning.

If you have a rush nighttime job (brought to them after 4 P.M.) and you need this work by the following morning, it is imperative that a member of your department stay with the night printing crew until the job is completed. In order to have a night rush job printed, your supervisor must initial a special Night Printing Form (available from the printing department).

11 COMPANY RULES AND REGULATIONS

Code of Conduct

List your expectations for your employees concerning their behavior during work hours.

We pride ourselves on the clean, orderly, safe, and healthy environment we've created at Montana. To continue this, we need your cooperation. Please read and follow these rules of conduct:

We prohibit fighting; abuse or destruction of property; possession of narcotics and weapons on the premises; falsification of company records; illegal, immoral, or indecent conduct or language; and removal from the premises of company property.

We do not allow employees to post notices anywhere without the permission of the personnel department.

We ask that employees not conduct personal business on company time or with company equipment and resources.

We stress an atmosphere of respect for each other's rights and privacy.

Smoking

List your smoking rules and regulations and specify non-smoking areas.

Employees may not smoke in the following areas:

Hallways

Elevators

Printing department

Photo lab

Nonsmoking area of the cafeteria

Personal Calls and Mail

State company policy with regard to personal phone calls and personal mail.

We ask that you limit your personal phone calls to emergencies or very important matters and that you keep these calls short. If you must make a long-distance personal call, please do not use the WATS line. Call the operator and give him or her your name and phone extension as well as the number you are calling. You will be billed for these calls at the end of each month, and are required to pay these bills within a month's time. Failure to pay your personal phone bills in time will prevent you from receiving your paycheck on time.

Our mailroom struggles to maintain a smooth-running operation and processes an enormous load of business mail and packages daily. We insist that you do not mail anything personal through the mailroom. We do not allow employees to use company postage for their personal mail. The nearest post office is located on Sixth Avenue and 60th Street and is easily accessible during your lunch hour.

Safety Regulations

List any special safety rules and regulations. Pay special attention to problem areas in your company, such as the factory area, parking lot, etc.

We expect that mature and responsible employees will follow basic rules of safety appropriate to large work areas for the health and protection of themselves, their colleagues, and their company. There are a few policies we would like to specify:

1. Do not try to lift and carry anything heavy by yourself. If you need assistance, call the mailroom.

2. Report any injury—large or small—to your supervisor or department secretary. Should you have an injury or feel ill while at work, go directly to the nurse's office and ask the nurse to contact your supervisor.

3. Do not enter the printing press area or the photo lab without permission from the department secretary. If a secretary is not outside, press the outside buzzer and wait for someone to come out and let you in.

4. Should you notice something that seems like a safety hazard anywhere in the office, please report this to the personnel department immediately.

Right of Inspection

This statement is important to include if the company wants the right to inspect employee's personal property.

It is the right of this company to inspect lunch pails, lockers, desks, and other personal areas at any given time. Please cooperate with us on this matter, as it may be done for your protection.

Company Rules and Regulations/57

Visitors

Explain how visitors must be announced and whether personal visitors are permitted.

All visitors must sign in at the main reception area on the first floor. They must sign out when they leave the premises.

Any special rules for visitors or privileges allowed should be explained here.

Please let your supervisor know if you want a friend or relative to visit you during the workday.

Dress Code and Uniforms

State your dress code and standards. If they differ from job to job or department to department, explain that here.

Our dress code varies from job to job, from department to department, and sometimes even from day to day. We ask that you report to work dressed neatly and appropriately. Your supervisor will advise you as to the exact dress regulations for your department and job. We do not allow blue jeans, T-shirts or sneakers, except for production employees who are going to spend the day on location.

Explain if uniforms are required for any employees. If you offer any special services for uniforms, such as cleaning them or paying for them, explain these services.

Uniforms are worn by employees who work in the maintenance department, the cafeteria, the photo lab, and the printing department. These uniforms are paid for by the employees and can be purchased through the department secretary. The company cleans these uniforms at company expense each week. Bring soiled uniforms to Maintenance on Fridays between 5 and 6 P.M. You can pick up your cleaned uniforms on Monday mornings between 7 and 9 A.M. Make sure to write your name clearly in indelible ink on the inside of the collar of each uniform.

12 COMPANY BENEFITS

Group Plans

List the benefits offered by your company.

The following is a list of benefits offered to all employees:

- Medical and Dental Insurance
- Life and Accidental Death Benefits
- Business Travel Accident Insurance
- Disability
- Profit-Sharing and Stock-Bonus Retirement Plans
- Stock Purchase Plan
- Social Security
- Workmen's Compensation
- Unemployment Insurance

Companies usually prepare separate booklets (or obtain printed literature from their insurance companies) to detail each plan. Explain where to get these booklets and who to call with questions.

When you begin employment here, you will be given booklets that explain these plans in detail. If you need additional information or further explanations on any of these plans, please call the personnel department. Our company nurse will help you fill out insurance forms that relate to illness or accidents.

State which plans are company paid and which are employee paid.

Blue Cross, Blue Shield, Major Medical, dental, and Social Security benefits are a shared expense between the company and employees. These expenses are automatically deducted from your weekly paychecks. The company pays all expenses for unemployment insurance and workmen's compensation.

The basic contributory and noncontributory life, medical, and dental insurance plans are outlined in the table that follows. Disability is covered in a separate section of this handbook. The stock and retirement plans are explained after the insurance outline.

Company Benefits/59

Set up an easy-to-read chart for insurance plans.

Insurance Benefit Program

Noncontributory Plans

Type of Coverage	Amount of Coverage	Cost of Coverage	Payroll Deduction
1. Basic Group Term Life Insurance	$_____	Company Paid	No Deduction
2. Basic Accidental Death and Dismemberment	_____	Company Paid	No Deduction
3. Business Travel Accident Insurance	_____	Company Paid	No Deduction
4. Short-Term Disability a. Weekly Accident and Sickness	_____	Company Paid	No Deduction
b. Illness Payment Plan (per month)	_____	Company Paid	No Deduction

Contributory Plans

Type of Coverage	Amount of Coverage	Cost of Coverage	Payroll Deduction
1. Long-Term Disability	_____	_____	_____
2. Medical and Dental	_____	_____	_____
3. Optional Group Term Life Insurance	_____	_____	_____
4. Dependent Term Life Insurance	_____	_____	_____
5. Optional Accidental Death and Dismemberment	_____	_____	_____

Explain other plans so that employees can get a general understanding of them at a glance.

Profit-Sharing and Stock-Bonus Retirement Plans

The profit-sharing and stock-bonus retirement plans are designed to provide you and your beneficiaries with financial resources for your retirement. Since the plans are a vehicle for the distribution of corporate profits, all contributions are made by the company.

You are automatically enrolled in these plans on the July 1 or January 1 (whichever is closest) after you have worked for the company one year. The amount of cash and stock contributions is determined by the board of directors and is based on the company's earnings and profits for the year. You will be advised as to the amount at the end of each year.

Sample Employee Handbook

> State what facilities are available to employees in case of illness or accident. Be specific about who is in charge, how a doctor can be reached, and where health office is located.
>
> If your company pays part or all of an employee's tuition for further education, explain how this works and how to apply for assistance.
>
> If you offer any in-house courses, explain what they are, where they are given, and how to apply or sign up.

Stock Purchase Plan

Montana provides you with the opportunity to invest in the company's growth and prosperity through the Employee Stock Purchase Plan. You may participate on the March 1 or September 1 following six months' of employment. The maximum value of your stock purchase is 10% of your total compensation for the preceding six months of employment. Your stock purchase is paid for automatically through payroll deductions. You will receive a stock certificate for your purchased shares following each Stock Purchase Plan period.

Health Services

Montana maintains a full-time health services office with a registered nurse on duty during regular working hours. In addition, a company doctor has offices in the building and is available when necessary. Our nurses are qualified to give first aid, as well as eye and hearing tests. If you have an accident while at work or do not feel well during your workday, report to the nurse's office on the second floor.

Tuition Assistance

The company offers tuition assistance to any employee who is interested in improving his or her job performance or bettering their potential for advancement. The company will pay 70% of tuition for job-related courses.

If you wish to receive tuition assistance, obtain an application from the personnel department and submit it before registering for any courses. Your supervisor must countersign the application.

In addition, Montana offers its own educational program of free seminars given by company employees who are expert in certain areas. These seminars are given on Wednesday nights from 6 to 8 P.M. in the large conference room on the third floor. Each seminar program lasts four weeks, and students are given a certificate of completion when they finish. Seminars are given on the following topics:

Finance
Art and Design for Communications
Copywriting
Film Production for Beginners
Personnel Procedures
How to Become an Account Executive
Supervisory Skills

Company Benefits /61

A schedule of these seminar courses is posted on the bulletin board outside Personnel. Sign-up sheets are available there as well. Students are chosen on a first-come, first-served basis. All courses are free to employees. Your supervisor may ask that you take one or several of these courses.

Company Loans

If your company makes pay advances or loans, explain here the amounts given, amount of time employee must have worked to apply, what forms must be filled out, what approval is expected, and how long it takes to get amount requested.

Montana Communications will advance up to four weeks of an employee's salary to help him or her meet an emergency.

Should you desire a company loan for the purpose of financing your car, home, or another reason, you may borrow an amount not to exceed $ _____ at _____ % interest. Loans are granted only to employees with two or more years of service.

To request a pay advance or to apply for a loan, fill out an application from the accounting department (Extension 23). Advances are granted immediately, once the appropriate forms are filled out and properly signed, but loan approval usually takes two to three weeks.

Explain repayment procedure.

A repayment schedule for an advance or loan is worked out at the time it is granted. Employees must sign loan agreements and pay back the loans on time.

13 SPECIAL SERVICES

Food Service

Explain company food services available—coffee carts, cafeterias, and dining rooms, and the hours and offerings of each.

There are carts stationed at the elevators during breaks that sell coffee, tea, milk, juices, fruit, bagels, Danish, rolls, and muffins. In addition, should you wish some privacy or need to walk around during your break, the cafeteria is open from 9:30 to 11 A.M. and from 3 to 4 P.M. The cafeteria's coffee-break menu includes yogurt, small salads, fruit cup, puddings, and soups, as well as everything offered on the carts.

The cafeteria serves lunch from noon until 2 P.M. each day. The menu varies daily and features attractive, nutritionally balanced, and inexpensive lunches, prepared by our dietitian and her staff. The cafeteria is company-owned and run as a nonprofit service to our employees. The cafeteria also offers a special diet plan. You may join the plan by calling our dietitian on Extension 127 and making an appointment to meet with her to discuss your special diet and goals.

We love our cafeteria! Please help us to continue to run it successfully by keeping it neat.

Welfare Committee

Describe this committee's function, who takes part, whether officials are elected or appointed, how employees become members, who serves as chairperson.

The Welfare Committee was started five years ago to further promote understanding and harmony between management and employees. It consists of twelve elected representatives, six of whom are members of management, and is chaired by one of the company's senior vice-presidents. Elections for these positions are held each December. No person may serve on this committee more than one year out of five.

This group meets monthly and discusses any matters that relate to the general welfare of the employees, including complaints and problems; social, recreational and educational activities; and safety and health issues. If you have an issue or idea you believe should be discussed by this committee, please put your suggestion in the Welfare Committee Suggestion Box, located outside the cafeteria.

If you are interested in serving on this committee, please submit your name in November to the present chairperson. Your supervisor must approve your participation on this committee, as meetings take place during the workday.

Service Recognition

Say who receives service awards and when they are given out.

To give recognition and appreciation for long and loyal service, Montana presents service awards each year at the Christmas party. Employees receive these awards after completing five years of service, and then every five years thereafter.

Awards for special achievements and contributions also are handed out at the Christmas party.

Lost and Found

Tell employees where Lost and Found is located and when it is open.

The company lost and found department is located next door to the health services office on the second floor. Please bring any item of value you might find to this department. Report any lost item immediately to them as well. All items must be properly identified before being claimed. The department is open every morning from 8 to 10 and again in the afternoon from 5 to 6.

Parking Lot

If your company provides parking for employees, state who may park there, whether spots are assigned, and where visitors should park.

We have two parking lots at Montana: one for employees and one for visitors. The employee lot is located at the rear of the building. If you drive to work every day, you will be assigned a spot. Please do not use any other parking space—even for a few minutes. Call Personnel on Extension 46 to receive an assigned parking spot or to report a car in your space.

The visitors' parking lot is located directly in front of the building. Employees may not use this lot.

The handicapped spots in both lots should be used only by people with handicapped parking permits.

Special Benefits

List any special benefits you offer your employees, such as free products and services, discounts, gifts, etc. Tell them when these are available and the procedure to be followed.

We pass on to our employees special benefits and discounts offered by our clients. Our employees are entitled to discounts on air travel when they fly Hunter Airways anywhere within the United States. Four times a year, employees receive gift boxes of food products produced by American Products. All Barbara Kaye Cosmetics are available to our employees at a 15% discount at J.R. Ford's Department Store. In order to receive this discount you must show your employee discount card (given you by the personnel department when you join the company). You will be offered sales and discounts several times a year on Trylon Electronics and Computer products.

List company teams and explain how interested employees can join.	# Recreational Activities

Montana Communications has the following company teams:

    Volleyball
    Baseball
    Bowling
    Basketball |
List other recreational activities and tell employees how they may participate. Explain the amount of time required and who to contact if they want to join.	These teams participate in the Advertising League of New York competitions. Please contact a Welfare Committee representative if you're interested in joining a team. The teams meet approximately twice a week to practice. All teams are coed. In addition, we have an active runners club and aerobic exercise group. The runners club meets every Monday, Wednesday, and Thursday morning at 7:30 in front of the building—rain or shine, hot weather or cold. Members run for about 40 minutes and are permitted to use the locker rooms and showers at the Y.M.H.A. located across the street. The aerobics classes are part of the Y's program. We will pay for an employee's class fees if the employee takes a minimum of three (maximum of four) classes a week. These coed classes are 45 minutes long and are offered weekdays at 7:30 A.M. and 12:15 P.M. Employees may use the Y's locker rooms and showers after class as well.
State whether you require a doctor's note or provide a company-paid physical.	Each employee who joins a team or program must have a physical with our company physician. Call Health Services to make these arrangements.
	# Company Parties and Events
Tell your employees what parties or special days the company sponsors, when these are held, and what goes on. Explain when they will receive further details about these events. Discuss other social functions they may be required to attend.	Montana Communications has two yearly celebrations for employees and their spouses. The first is our annual July 4th picnic in Mountain Park. This picnic is for all employees and their immediate families. We offer a gourmet lunch, musical entertainment, and games and contests for everyone. You will get a memo explaining this special day at least three weeks beforehand. Our Christmas party is usually held at the St. Todd Hotel one week before the Christmas holidays. It is a festive evening of food and dance. Each employee may bring his or her spouse or a friend if they wish. You will receive an invitation to this party about a month in advance. In addition, we are constantly planning and taking part in our clients' product introductions, parties, celebrations, and events. You will be notified as to the dates of any functions in which your participation is expected.
State company policy on employee parties.	Employees' birthdays, anniversaries, weddings, retirements, and similar celebrations are planned at the discretion of each department and the department supervisor.

14 SPECIAL POLICIES

For Film Production Department Employees Only

This is an example of sections you might want to include only for the employees of a specific department when their rules are different from normal company policy. These sections can be handed out to employees by the personnel department or department supervisor and put into their company manual at the back. In these sections, it is important to list each regulation that is different from the norm. Make sure to be very specific.

Our department has several policies that vary from normal company policy. It is important for you to familiarize yourselves with these variations immediately upon joining this department. They are as follows:

1. Our regular hours are 9 A.M. to 5 P.M. Mondays through Thursdays. On Fridays we begin our workday at 8 A.M., at which time we hold an hour-long department meeting. The workday on Friday ends at 4 P.M. These hours are followed by employees when they are working in the office, not when they are on location or out of town.

2. Film production department employees do not receive overtime. Because of this, salaries have been adjusted to reflect the additional hours required.

3. Employees follow the general company dress code when working in the office. On location, the technical staff may wear jeans, T-shirts, and sneakers. Producers and directors are expected to dress professionally when dealing with the clients, even on the set.

PART 4
REPRODUCIBLE HANDBOOK PAGES

ABOUT THE COMPANY

HOW WE ARE ORGANIZED

JOINING US

LEAVING US

EVALUATIONS, WARNINGS, AND PROBATION

COMPANY COMMUNICATIONS

YOUR SALARY

DAYS AND HOURS OF WORK

TIME OFF

COMPANY PROCEDURES

COMPANY RULES AND REGULATIONS

COMPANY BENEFITS

SPECIAL SERVICES

SPECIAL POLICIES